05/23
$2.50

The Light Comes Slowly

*For my dear friend Augie,
In this case, less is definately more;
short poems for your enjoyment.
— Kathleen
Christmas '98*

*As I was at three
I seem to be at eighty
serene and thankful.*

The Light Comes Slowly
Short poems from Kyoto

by Edith Shiffert

Sumi Illustrations
by Kohka Saito

Katsura Press
1997

Publications by Edith Shiffert

Original Poetry
  In Open Woods
  For a Return to Kona
  The Kyoto Years
  A Grasshopper
  New & Selected Poems
  A Way to Find Out
  Kyoto Dwelling
  Forest House With Cat
  When at the Edge
  Clean Water with Minoru Sawano

Translations
  Anthology of Modern Japanese Poetry with Yuki Sawa
  Chieko by Kotaro Takamura
  When a Bird Rests & Other Tanka by Taeko Takaori
  Haiku Master Buson with Yuki Sawa

Published by Katsura Press
P. O. Box 275
Lake Oswego, OR 97034

Copyright © 1997
by Katsura Press

All rights reserved

Library of Congress Catalog Card No. 96-79913
International Standard Book No. 0-9638551-6-6

Printed on recycled, acid-free paper

To Minoru Sawano
who has been experiencing this life
since March 1911

Preface

Thirty years at Kyoto's gates without once knocking.
I used to believe it was because of having climbed
all the surrounding hills that this was home.
An accumulated knowledge too:
knowing in which hollow certain flowers would be—
white rhododendron at the north side of a ridge
wild peonies farther up a stream just
before it became a waterfall.

With fading sight, hearing, memory, motion
empathy becomes strong and sufficient.
As a heavy winged heron returns to a certain tree
after a short absence or a long one, ways are found
across open spaces to the habitual,
not just by remembrance but inevitability.

I will find again what was often sought—
a trembling of wings on long flights
and the continued going.

> *The sky is all black*
> *then light comes slowly, slowly*
> *while the cat watches.*

Edith Shiffert
Kyoto, Japan 1997

January

Again the ancient plum,
New Year, Tanizaki's grave—
only four blossoms.

January

The new year begins
with the same sun overhead
and the same hiyo-bird.

Who will tell me where
I will walk to this year
on unstable legs?

Does such a blue sky
foretell a new year of peace?
Sparrows at their crumbs.

January

Carefully the cat
steps onto the snowy walk.
Darkness and whiteness!

A few ice crystals
between old rocks in the pond.
Fish and ducks break through.

January

The shaman I am
was here since my beginning.
Let it stay with me.

Turning of aeons
and the changing of moments.
Are they both the same?

Today Daimon-ji
is white on its upper half.
A hawk swoops downward.

January

While being vital
find a place to rest yourself—
narcissus in snow!

Looking for myself
I find a pair of old glasses.
I can see with them!

January

All those multitudes
who died alone and silent!
Why do I feel joy?

If I were a cat
I too would be out tonight
in the snowy dark.

Now it is winter,
crows take bread with the pigeons
all of them hungry.

January

I know the cold wind
and the warm things that will come
as the new year grows.

Though it is winter
tonight's full moon is misty.
Scent of narcissus.

February

Drooping lotus pods
on the pond, carp still drowsy,
the turtles hidden.

February

Gently but quickly
feathers of snow coming down
so darkness is white.

One hungry sparrow
has already found the crumbs
hiyo-bird asked for.

February

Though seen half my life
still I will look for Kyoto's
fragrant plum blossoms.

Cat runs home to eat
then quickly back to his friends.
Kittens in two months?

Some say Buddhism
is a way of discipline.
Cat watching the sky?

February

Pray to nothingness.
Oh pray, for it is coming.
The clouds drift away.

An internal fire
brings steam from the bird's throat
and the air takes it.

February

Is the cat snoring
or the old man? Both asleep.
Winter afternoon.

The black dog on guard
and the white cat by my feet
show me what I am.

From the balcony
cat watches snowflakes falling.
Only ten p.m.

February

Wall tops and pavements
only damp from constant snow.
Where did it go?

You and you and you
I have known intimately.
Just this feeling left.

February

Snow and wind last night;
now sunshine, and the bamboos
tossing and tossing.

Oh Kannon, appear
as an affectionate cat
and lie close to me.

One small heap of snow
gritty beside the bus stop.
Winter almost gone.

March

All these camellias
opening and falling down.
Nijo's moat with swans.

March

Old man on the floor
kneels pressed against the heater
studying haiku.

Shadows of bamboo
vibrate across the window.
A quick bird shadow!

Our silly old age
makes every flower lovely,
every dog a friend.

March

Why is it joyous
to walk under plum blossoms
though the wind is cold?

Too eager, the gull
flies right down onto my hand
for a bit of bread.

March

That camellia poised
white upon its smooth black branch;
now it will drop down.

Assurance of bliss—
broken body, broken trees
filled with blossoming.

My feet are freezing
while I scald my mouth with tea.
Late spring in Kyoto.

March

Praising as I climbed
all the beloved mountains
each a way of rocks.

Too old for climbing
I look at my flower books,
spring in the mountains.

March

The cat has eaten
and the birds in the garden
and we have eaten.

Today no cold wind
and plum petals do not fall.
Fragrance in sunshine.

That Zen monk also
nine months inside his mother.
Salted plum with rice.

March

Journey almost done
we sit relaxed side by side
with an old white cat.

Thank you for your care
old man tells the old woman
now that winter's gone.

April

Curves of temple roofs
and boughs of the old cherry trees.
Upcurve of bird wings.

April

Ancient cedar trees
by clouds of cherry blossoms.
Pray the world can last.

Buddhas are nothing
and I am nothing also.
So then what are we?

April

Shadows of sparrows
flitting across the pavement—
real birds overhead.

Sunlight comes slowly
across the front room carpet
while nothing else moves.

With the entire earth
drenched in flowers and fragrance
why not peace and joy?

April

Two abandoned cats
wash each other's white faces
where a pathway turns.

Fragrance of incense
by Yoshida-yama's graves.
Pine needles sparkle.

April

Now as my life ends
to walk beneath these cherries
on and on and on!

We and the cherries
both almost finished but yet
out in the sunshine.

In these ditches too
fallen petals of cherries,
the outcastes' district.

April

Old age loneliness,
knowing death really happens
and many have gone.

The lake lies quiet
between the forested hills.
Purple azaleas.

April

Climbing on lava
upward for thousands of feet
remembered as joy.

How does ninety feel?
Not different from sixteen
my mother always said.

Is this joy senile?
Let be, let be, no matter.
Another new moon!

May

Flashes of silver
as small fish jump through water
inside the river.

May

Because I cannot
use stepping stones or bridge,
I take the long path.

A shrine turtle swims
between white water lilies
carrying himself.

This quiet landscape
filled itself with a forest,
the trees with songbirds.

May

Think of what we are
and the trees and the river.
Walk the simple way.

One bit of blue sky
then clouds over the city
twelve hundred years old.

May

She walks heavily
carrying her unborn child.
We, because of age.

To forgetfulness
I give all my consciousness.
Cat knows what to do.

The cat nips my ear
and I tell him we are not
such good friends as that.

May

The way the pine trees
tall and thin lean from the hills!
One last cherry tree.

The pain of the world
not washed away by rivers
nor blown off by winds.

May

Body fed to birds,
body having fed on birds.
The substance the same.

Oh I am zestful
in this field of grasses
openmouthed for rain.

The first time this spring
to hear frog voices chanting,
rain on rocks and moss.

May

Communicating
with the eager cat all day—
food, naps, in and out.

Oh those clouds, those clouds,
are they a sea or a sky?
Colors change to night.

June

Hiyo-bird leans down
from a branch and calls to me,
no bread in summer?

June

Seen for eighty years
but still I feel awed and glad—
white water lilies.

Cat washes her face
after eating the trap bait.
It was delicious!

June

Full of bliss and clear
my mind was in the mountains.
Ferns by waterfalls.

Just to live too long
the biggest joke of all.
But is it too long?

In a mountain field
I wait for death. An ox eats
flowers, licks my face.

June

After days of constant rain
the moon just discernible
beyond all the haze.

In the far north, lakes
shone with light for entire nights.
The trumpeting swans!

June

Broad wings of the hawk
barely move as he comes down
into the garden.

I want you here friend
by the garden where we talked.
Can one dead know that?

While carp keep splashing,
rain on the water lilies
and rain on my face.

June

The tired old man
hikes uphill in summer heat
for his injection.

From cup or hand
water has the same cool taste.
Drink and be thankful.

June

The way of the cat
lures me still farther onward.
Have I had enough?

Before the great change
lie at ease upon the earth—
soon you will have it.

In new deep grasses
under the shade of the trees,
Moooooo!

July

The brown ducks floating
on the Kamo River move
only their two feet.

July

Neck-deep in flowers
trust in the Buddha nature
for just this one day.

Not raining, not clear,
the leaves are all glistening
in the pure darkness.

Seen past bamboo leaves
a softly blurred full round moon.
First night without rain.

July

Over rocks and down
to where the ducks are resting,
water in the heat.

This meditation
continuing on and on
fulfills all hungers.

July

Just being joyful
though alone in a stillness.
This, eternity?

Like water lilies
or a quiet cat lounging,
this body of bliss.

God-being within
my self and traveling birds
sustains our flying.

July

Heat takes the leaves
one by one they droop and drop,
the branches half bare.

White owl on my wrist
weeks ago, the weightless touch,
cool feathers and feet.

July

Adoring the cat
or the man becomes the same.
Both of them Buddhas.

Here in the quiet
before rain pours down again,
I remember years.

For this small beetle
a lifetime on one tree trunk.
Everything is there.

July

Wherever it is
one can get there finally—
the cats can go too.

Gratitude for sight
of all things that have being.
Their mysteries!

August

Pink lotus flowers.
I fold my hands to their shape
and want a Buddha.

August

Scent of grass and pines
through the screaming of locusts.
I am awake now.

Red begonia
dangling from a flower pot—
the bee has found it.

August

The departed cat
still seems to be everywhere
as he was before.

What can be found in
the simple and natural?
Relax while looking.

The trees accept rain
after a long time of drought,
every leaf refreshed.

August

In heavy rainfall
from under umbrellas,
Daimon-ji's burning.

Our cats dead a month,
their relatives come tonight
and peer through the screens.

August

A crystal of water
centered on a lotus leaf.
The end of Obon.

The din of insects
while we perspire all day long.
I too feel cranky.

He sleeps a little
with two-hour drip injections.
Summer hospital.

August

Only a few birds
fly by in this heavy heat.
Ducks sleep on water.

My father's question:
What happens after we die?
Soon I will find out.

August

I rest on the steps
but cannot rise up alone.
View with camphor trees.

Finding no pathway
I find myself in heavens
moment by moment.

Water in a vase
on the table, cat drinking.
The end of August.

September

Equinox lilies
fading just after blooming.
Fields of red tatters.

September

Water in the ditches
the sound of Nanzen-ji
how lightly it flows.

This, too, sentient
the firm rock on the pathway
where I have stumbled?

All I can say is
I see and am satisfied.
Big mountain. Dark night.

September

Not being a monk
but feeling as though I were,
without a belief.

The body of bliss
goes away at a light push.
The body of pain!

September

Now that I am old
I remember being young
as though nothing changed.

That old ginkgo tree,
the longer I look at it
the more I am it.

With just today's rain
the season changed to autumn.
The coolness of air!

September

The minute insects
slowly creeping up the wall.
Do they have a name?

Over tall cedars
a crow goes flying swiftly
toward the thick black clouds.

September

Resting on the earth
who needs satori or faith?
Embrace what holds you!

A small piece of sky,
only that from the window,
but with this sunset!

Quickly getting dark—
fast movements of the bamboos
slowly disappear.

September

While eating a mouse
the cat yawns and looks away.
The moon just came up.

A winter futon
on the bed after summer.
Cat leaps onto it!

October

A small narrow moon
caught upon the bamboo stems.
Evening chill.

October

    Seagulls have returned
and riverside goldenrod.
Another year gone.

    Joy comes back to him
after the long hot summer.
The happy old man!

October

No plans for autumn—
it will come naturally
like these plumed grasses.

Warmth of the sunshine
relaxes all our muscles.
Gravel on the paths.

With the autumn leaves
a butterfly too is blown
across our pathway.

October

All along the street
branches have been pruned back
just before bright leaves.

Dropped onto the walk
small blooms of Russian olives.
My shoes are perfumed.

October

Three years since he died
but this morning white cat hairs
on an old sweater.

Beside a park pond
a bar hostess and her friend
drink morning saké.

Banks of cosmos
swaying in the cool sunlight.
End of October.

October

Home from the market
I realize that my teeth
are still on the shelf.

The praying mantis
lost on balcony flowers
will find only frost.

October

My friend's husband dead
and a lost bird at the eaves
chirping all day long.

Even in the room
shadows are leaping about—
trees in autumn wind.

Poplar or maple
backyard trees move the same,
Detroit or Japan.

November

Out under red leaves
Shinnyo-do's black bronze Buddha.
Has it compassion?

November

Can I feel the bliss
of the scarlet leaves and sky
and myself quiet?

Ryôkan too
would have liked these gaudy hills.
Kyoto November.

No turtles today
but the carp eat the bread crumbs—
cold and shallow pond!

November

The happy old man
also writes in a notebook.
This autumn sunshine!

Just beyond the wall
tree still half full of red leaves
and our lives still here.

November

Large white lilies now
for our marriage twelve years past.
Their heavy, sweet scent!

Food tangled in teeth
legs going wrong directions
I rise from my chair.

Be still now, be still.
See the sunlight on your hands
and on air, your breath.

November

Walking through red leaves
then napping with a white cat.
How else to grow old?

My soul is sleepy
but purring like an old cat
curled up in winter.

November

The river flows through
its own reflections of light
while white herons watch.

Winter coat today
and light snow on the ridges—
the city not changed.

Husband with shingles
wife with a heavy head cold
laugh while the cat plays.

November

We trust each other
cat and I. Inside his yawn
I put a finger.

All these years the cat
washes and washes himself.
Still not clean enough.

December

The crow comes closer
flapping along under pines.
Sounds of far-off winds.

December

I feel my spirit
glowing in a dark forest
like the last red leaves.

The happy old man
a bit grumpy in winter—
new heater soothes him.

December

This comic old age
I laugh at it heartily
—hands, feet, eyes, ears, teeth?

Clippings in a bowl
or a whole hedge of fragrance
cedar, ever green.

As we and the world
turn to another new year,
oh pray for us, pray!

December

Two herons soar by,
then fifty gulls float on air.
I feel my wings too.

The happy old man
lies on his bed in sunlight.
The swaying bamboo.

December

Only an hour left
but think of other years gone
and those not yet come.

Patterns blown on snow
shift and reform and reform.
To see is joyous.

Outside in the cold
a few gnats at the window.
Still alive tonight?

December

    Just now as we change
    from one year to another,
    I remember you.

    Cat watches in awe
    as the couch changes again
    into a big bed.

December

In the cold I sleep
one hand on the cat's belly
and one on my own.

The body of bliss
warms us before departure.
Is there still more light?

On my final walk
I look carefully for
whatever is there.

I would like to thank the following people for their assistance in the creation of this book:
Betsy Benjamin
Margaret Chula
Judith Clancy
John Hall
Kohka Saito
Stephen Suloway
Yumiko Ueno

Edith Shiffert was born in Toronto, Canada in 1916, but after the age of three lived in the United States, including remote parts of Hawaii and Alaska. From 1956 to 1962 she was a student at the University of Washington in the Department of East Asian Studies, Anthropology and Creative Writing. She is a founder and former editor of *Poetry Northwest*. Since 1963 she has resided in Kyoto, Japan, where she was a professor at Doshisha University and Kyoto Seika College until her retirement. Her poetry has been widely published in periodicals such as the *New Yorker* and *Saturday Review*. She has received numerous awards, including first prize in the prestigious JAL/Mainichi haiku contest.

Kohka Saito was born in Kyoto in 1930 and spent his early years in China. He became accomplished in the techniques of traditional Japanese painting under the tutelage of two of Kyoto's great masters, Osho Maruyama and Raicho Takahashi. *The Tale of Genji* and Chinese landscapes are the major themes of his work, which has been commissioned for Buddhist temples and shown at annual exhibitions. He illustrated Edith Shiffert's poems for *Kyoto Dwelling* and designed and illustrated her *Forest House with Cat*. In 1992 *Arts of Asia* featured his work and honored him as a unique living traditional artist in Japan.

THE LIGHT COMES SLOWLY
Designed by John Hall and Margaret Chula
Composed by John Hall
in Palatino
Printed by Gilliland Printing, Inc.
on Springhill Cream stock